Literature Review of Colorimetric Indicators for Nerve-Agent Detection

H. Dupont Durst

NIMBLE BOOKS LLC: THE AI LAB FOR BOOK-LOVERS

~ FRED ZIMMERMAN, EDITOR ~

Humans and AI making books richer, more diverse, and more surprising.

Publishing Information

(c) 2024 Nimble Books LLC
ISBN: 978-1-60888-280-9

AI-generated Keyword Phrases

colorimetric indicators; nerve-agent detection; literature review; introduction; mechanisms of action; two-step processes; false-positive results; selectivity improvement; organophosphorus compounds testing; test strips development; low-cost screening method; rapid screening method

Publisher's Notes

This document provides a literature review of colorimetric indicators for nerve-agent detection, offering valuable insights into the development and use of these indicators. By reading this document, readers can gain a deeper understanding of the potential applications and benefits of colorimetric indicators in detecting nerve agents. Given the current public concerns regarding chemical warfare and the need for effective detection methods, this document offers relevant and timely information for researchers, policymakers, and security agencies.

This annotated edition illustrates the capabilities of the AI Lab for Book-Lovers to add context and ease-of-use to manuscripts. It includes several types of abstracts, building from simplest to more complex: TLDR (one word), ELI5, TLDR (vanilla), Scientific Style, and Action Items; essays to increase viewpoint diversity, such as Grounds for Dissent, Red Team Critique, and MAGA Perspective; and Notable Passages and Nutshell Summaries for each page.

On a personal note, this document struck a chord because my grandfather and namesake, William Zimmerman III, was a chemist who shared a patent for a colorimetric temperature indicator.

United States Patent [19]

Smith et al.

[11] **3,786,777**

[45] **Jan. 22, 1974**

[54] **IRREVERSIBLE WARM-UP INDICATOR**

[75] Inventors: **Robert W. Smith,** Oakton, Va.; **Fred Ordway,** Bethesda, Md.; **Charles A. Taylor,** Falls Church; **William Zimmerman, III,** Alexandria, both of Va.

[73] Assignee: **Artech Corporation,** Falls Church, Va.

[22] Filed: **Dec. 31, 1970**

[21] Appl. No.: **103,146**

[52] U.S. Cl. .... **116/114 AB**
[51] Int. Cl. .... **A23 , G01d 21/00**
[58] Field of Search...... 99/192 TI, 211; 116/114 V, 116/114 Y, 114 AM, 114 AB; 73/356; 23/253 R

Primary Examiner—Norman Yudkoff
Assistant Examiner—Kenneth P. Van Wyck
Attorney, Agent, or Firm—Brufsky, Staas, Breiner and Halsey

[57] **ABSTRACT**

An indicator for use with a refrigerated object to indicate visually that the object has rewarmed and to warn of possible spoilage. The indicator includes a transparent package housing a frangible container filled with a liquid that expands on freezing and an indicator material placed in proximity thereto which will undergo a color change when contacted by the liquid. The liquid freezes when refrigerated along with the object and expands fracturing the container which previously prevented communication between the liquid and indicator material. Rewarming of the object causes the liquid to melt and contact the indicator material to re-

He worked for a startup that sought to commercialize this technology. While it was not successful, it was a valiant effort.

(William) Fred(erick) Zimmerman (V)
Ann Arbor, Michigan, USA

Annotations

ABSTRACTS

TL;DR (ONE WORD)

Colorimetric.

EXPLAIN IT TO ME LIKE I'M FIVE YEARS OLD

This document is like a special book that talks about how to use colors to find dangerous chemicals called nerve agents. Nerve agents are things that can make people very sick or even hurt them. The book explains different ways to use colors to find these nerve agents and how they work. It also talks about making sure the colors only show up when there really is a nerve agent and not by mistake. The book also talks about testing different chemicals and making special paper with colors on it to find the nerve agents

TL;DR (VANILLA)

This document reviews colorimetric indicators for detecting nerve agents. It discusses different indicators, their mechanisms, and the use of two-step processes to improve accuracy. It also mentions testing different compounds and developing test strips with indicators. Overall, colorimetric indicators show promise as a low-cost and rapid method for screening nerve agents.

SCIENTIFIC STYLE

This literature review focuses on colorimetric indicators for the detection of nerve agents. The document provides an introduction to the topic and explores different colorimetric indicators and their mechanisms of action. It highlights the use of two-step processes to enhance selectivity and reduce false-positive results. The review also discusses the testing of various organophosphorus compounds and the development of test strips embedded with colorimetric indicators. Overall, it emphasizes the potential of colorimetric indicators as a cost-effective and rapid screening method for detecting nerve agents.

ACTION ITEMS

Further research on the development of colorimetric indicators for nerve-agent detection, including new mechanisms of action and improved selectivity.

Explore the use of two-step processes in colorimetric indicator systems to enhance accuracy and reduce false-positive results.

Investigate the testing of different organophosphorus compounds to expand the range of detectable nerve agents.

Explore the potential of embedding colorimetric indicators into test strips for easy and portable detection.

Consider the cost-effectiveness and feasibility of implementing colorimetric indicators as a screening method for nerve-agent detection in various settings.

VIEWPOINTS

These perspectives increase the reader's exposure to viewpoint diversity.

GROUNDS FOR DISSENT

A member of the organization responsible for this document might have principled, substantive reasons to dissent from this report for several reasons:

Lack of comprehensive literature review: The document may not cover all relevant studies and findings on colorimetric indicators for nerve-agent detection. If the member believes that important research or alternative approaches have been overlooked, they may dissent due to concerns about the report's completeness and accuracy.

Insufficient evidence for effectiveness: The document might rely on limited or inconclusive evidence regarding the efficacy of colorimetric indicators in detecting nerve agents. If the member has access to contradictory research or doubts about the reliability of the cited studies, they may dissent based on concerns about the validity and generalizability of the report's conclusions.

Bias towards low-cost solutions: The document appears to emphasize the potential of colorimetric indicators as a low-cost screening method. However, if the member believes that other detection methods (e.g., spectroscopy or mass spectrometry) offer higher sensitivity or reliability despite being more expensive, they may dissent due to concerns about prioritizing cost over accuracy.

Potential limitations of two-step processes: While the document highlights two-step processes to reduce false-positive results and enhance selectivity, a dissenting member might argue that these additional steps could introduce complexity or delays in detection protocols. They may question whether the benefits outweigh potential drawbacks and advocate for simpler, one-step approaches instead.

Limited scope of testing organophosphorus compounds: If the document does not adequately address variations among different organophosphorus compounds or their potential impact on colorimetric indicator performance, a dissenting member may argue that such oversights undermine the report's applicability and relevance to real-world scenarios. They may call for further investigation into compound-specific interactions with indicators.

Practical limitations of test strip implementation: The mention of test strips embedded with colorimetric indicators suggests a potentially practical application for nerve-agent detection. However, a dissenting member might raise concerns about the feasibility of mass production, storage, and distribution of these test strips. They may question whether alternative formats or technologies could offer more practical solutions.

Overall, a principled and substantive dissent from this document might arise from concerns about its comprehensiveness, evidence base, potential bias, limitations of proposed processes or tests, and practical considerations regarding implementation. The dissenting member would likely argue for further research, expanded investigations, or alternative approaches to ensure comprehensive and reliable nerve-agent detection methods.

RED TEAM CRITIQUE

The document on colorimetric indicators for nerve-agent detection provides a thorough introduction to the topic and effectively discusses different indicators and their mechanisms of action. The inclusion of various organophosphorus compounds in testing adds credibility to the research.

One strength of the document is its emphasis on two-step processes that aim to reduce false-positive results and improve selectivity. This approach demonstrates a thoughtful consideration of potential limitations and challenges associated with colorimetric indicators. Additionally, the discussion on embedded test strips underscores the practicality and convenience of this method, further enhancing its potential as a rapid screening tool.

However, there are some areas where the document could benefit from improvement. Firstly, while there is mention of different indicator types, such as dyes and nanoparticles, more specific details would enhance understanding for readers unfamiliar with these technologies. Providing examples or case studies showcasing each type's effectiveness would also strengthen arguments for their usefulness in nerve-agent detection.

Additionally, expanding upon existing limitations or drawbacks associated with colorimetric indicators would add balance to the overall analysis. Discussing factors such as environmental conditions (e.g., temperature or humidity) that may affect indicator reliability would give readers a comprehensive view.

Furthermore, it could be beneficial to address potential vulnerabilities in this screening method that adversaries might exploit. By identifying weaknesses or countermeasures that could potentially undermine accurate detection results, readers can better grasp both advantages and limitations when considering implementation.

In terms of organization, it may be useful to restructure the content so that information flows more logically from one concept to another. Clear section headings can guide readers through distinct subtopics within colorimetric indicator research specifically related to nerve-agent detection.

Finally, providing recommendations for future research directions or areas needing further investigation could inspire additional scientific exploration into improving current methods' efficacy or developing novel approaches altogether.

Overall, this literature review presents an informative overview of colorimetric indicators for detecting nerve agents but could benefit from more specific explanations regarding indicator types and their efficacy. It should also address vulnerabilities in the screening method and consider reorganizing content for improved clarity. With these revisions, the document would become an even more valuable resource within this field of study.

MAGA Perspective

This document is just another example of the liberal elite's obsession with unnecessary and wasteful research. Why are we wasting taxpayer dollars studying colorimetric indicators for nerve-agent detection? This is just another attempt by the deep state to distract us from the real issues facing our country.

Furthermore, the document's mention of two-step processes and reducing false-positive results shows a clear bias towards political correctness. We should be focused on efficiency and accuracy, not worrying about hurting someone's feelings or being selective. The fact that they prioritize selectivity over getting accurate results is deeply concerning.

Additionally, testing different organophosphorus compounds seems like a complete waste of time. We already know that nerve agents are dangerous and shouldn't be used. Why do we need to spend hours in a lab testing different variants? It's obvious that these researchers have too much time on their hands and no real understanding of what matters to hardworking Americans.

And don't get me started on these so-called "test strips embedded with colorimetric indicators." This is just another way for the government to invade our privacy and infringe upon our rights as citizens. We should be focusing on securing our borders and protecting American jobs, not developing invasive surveillance tools.

Overall, this document represents everything that is wrong with modern academia and scientific research. It prioritizes unnecessary studies over practical solutions for everyday Americans. It's time to put an end to this wasteful spending and focus on what truly matters - making America great again!

PAGE-BY-PAGE SUMMARIES

BODY-1   *This page is a literature review of colorimetric indicators for nerve-agent detection conducted by the U.S. Army Combat Capabilities Development Command Chemical Biological Center.*

BODY-2   *This page contains a disclaimer stating that the findings of the report should not be considered as an official position of the Department of the Army unless authorized by other documents.*

BODY-3   *This page is a report on a literature review of colorimetric and fluorescent indicators for detecting nerve agents.*

BODY-5   *The report describes work conducted by the U.S. Army on chemical and biological defense. It does not endorse any commercial products and is approved for public release.*

BODY-7   *The page discusses various methods of colorimetric and enzyme-based detection of nerve agents, including fluorophosphate and cyanophosphate detection, as well as synthetic carbon-based polymers. The conclusion is provided along with a list of literature cited.*

BODY-9   *Colorimetric indicators offer a simple and quick method to screen for nerve-agent material. A two-step process using fluorophosphate compounds has been developed to reduce false-positive results and increase selectivity in detecting nerve agents.*

BODY-10 *The page discusses a reaction pathway for Gil's two-step indicator and the use of a simulant to show that the leaving group from the initial reaction is unable to remove a specific group, resulting in a green solution.*

BODY-11 *A colorimetric indicator involving diisopropyl fluorophosphate (DFP) shows promise as a potential detector for fluorine-containing OP compounds such as sarin and soman. It exhibits good selectivity and can determine approximate concentration by color intensity.*

BODY-12 *The page discusses the synthesis and reaction pathways of colorimetric indicators for detecting tabun and related compounds. It highlights the unexpected relocation of the phosphate group in the reaction and the use of cyanide as a nucleophile to drive the reaction towards a more thermodynamically stable product.*

BODY-13 *New nerve-agent sensors have been developed that can detect and detoxify toxic compounds. These sensors undergo reactions that produce noticeable color changes, allowing for easy monitoring. Additionally, heavy-metal complexes are being explored for their use in optical sensory schemes.*

BODY-14 *The page discusses the development of a phosphorescence-based sensing system for cyanogen halides and a new selective method for detecting volatile phosphate esters using platinum complexes. It also mentions the use of boron dipyrromethene (BODIPY) as a framework for fluorescent dyes.*

BODY-15 *BODIPY dyes have potential for detecting chemical warfare agents. Two BODIPY dyes with basic nitrogen groups showed strong absorption and fluorescence, and low detection limits for nerve-agent simulants. Other BODIPY indicators selectively detected nerve-agent mimics with good limits of detection, even in the gas phase.*

BODY-16 *Research on BODIPY dyes focused on improving sensitivity and anchoring for detection of chemical agents. Dyes were covalently bound to a mesoporous silica and tested with nerve-agent mimics in vapor and water. Results showed measurable quenching of fluorescence and varying performance between mimics and nerve agents.*

NOTABLE PASSAGES

BODY-9   "A potential problem with using colorimetric indicators to detect nerve agents is that false-positive results may occur when a non-chemical warfare (CW) material triggers a color change. In 2011, Gotor et al.1 reported the first example of a molecule that reduces the possibility of a false positive by using a two-step process to trigger the color change (Figure 1). In the first step, the alcohol functional group nucleophilically attacks the phosphorus center of a fluorophosphate, causing the release of fluoride ions. An elimination reaction forms a more highly conjugated system, and the color changes to green (from the original clear solution). In a second step, the fluoride ions may react with the silicon atom of the tert-buty

BODY-11   "This molecule shows great promise as a potential detector for fluorine-containing OP compounds such as sarin and soman; or, depending on test results with actual agents, it may provide a good lead compound that can be optimized for these agents."

BODY-12   "The second step was surprising to the researchers as well as these authors. Although they expected to see a nucleophilic attack at one of the pyridine carbons or possibly at the azo linkage between the aromatic rings, the actual product was the one shown, in which the phosphate group has relocated to the aniline ring. The driving force for this reaction is not clear. It could be caused by the sterically less-hindered pyridine reaction taking place (for kinetic reasons), which would be irreversible for the non-cyanide-containing phosphates."

BODY-13   "Additionally, any detected nerve agent was detoxified upon reaction, thereby creating the potential for the construction of hybrid materials that not only detect the toxins but also simultaneously decompose them."

BODY-14   "The lack of solvent-polarity effect on the addition of BrCN suggests a radical mechanism. Oxidative addition of BrCN to the metal complexes in solution or dispersed in poly(methylmethacrylate) produced blue-shifted emissive Pt(IV) complexes. The blue-shifted products gave a dark-field sensing scheme that contrasted sharply with energy transfer-based sensing schemes."

BODY-15   "In 2014, Barba-Bon et al.10 reported the use of two BODIPY dyes as potential fluorescent and colorimetric indicators. A problem with some indicators is that they may yield a false-positive result when exposed to an acid.10 The two BODIPY dyes that were studied were formulated with basic nitrogen (pyridinyl) groups in the molecules and were reported to be less prone to this potential interference. Both dyes exhibited very strong absorption in the visible spectrum and strong fluorescence. Figure 8 shows the variant that exhibited the lowest detection limits for the nerve-agent simulants in acetonitrile solution: DCNP (0.1 ppm) and DFP (0.39 ppm)."

BODY-16   "In 2016 and 2017, Climent et al. reported that they had covalently bound BODIPY at an α-position to a mesoporous silica (SBA) functionalized with (aminopropyl)triethoxysilane (APTES) and had tested for responses to mimics and nerve agents in vapor12 and in water.13 The dyes all shared a trimethylphenyl at the meso position but had different functional groups at the remaining α positions."

BODY-18   "The molecule is small and relatively easy to produce. In a solution of as little as 50 mM (in a series of different solvents), the final solution was a visible light pink color, and it fluoresced strongly when excited by a 532 nm laser."

BODY-19   "Xuan et al.17 presented a new ratiometric fluorescent probe (Figure 14) that responds to DCP in less than 1 min at concentrations as low as 0.17 ppm. Color changes can also be seen under UV light or with the naked eye. This was the second fluorescent probe system to use Förster resonance energy transfer (FRET) in a ratiometric probe. FRET involves the transfer of energy from one chromophore to another through nonradiative dipole–dipole coupling. This probe responded to both vapor- and solution-phase agent simulants."

BODY-20   "For instance, fluorescent quenching, I/I0 = 0.68 (where I is the intensity after the quenching process and I0 is the initial intensity), was obtained when the sensor was exposed to 16 ppb of DCP."

BODY-21   "The successful detection of DCP suggested the utility of rhodamine deoxylactams as a chromofluorogenic signal-reporting platform for the design of sensors to target reactive chemical species via various chemistries."

BODY-22   "Climent et al.25 developed an approach for the chromogenic sensing of nerve-agent mimics by using silica nanoparticles (SNPs) that were functionalized with aliphatic alcohol and thiol moieties. When a solution of squaraine dye (SD) was added to a suspension of the functionalized SNPs, the reaction between the thiol moieties and the squaraine caused bleaching of the blue dye. However, when nerve-agent mimics were added to the hybrid SNP suspensions, the OP reacted with the hydroxyl groups of the alcohol moieties. This hindered the access of SD to the thiols of the SNPs, and the solutions remained blue."

BODY-23   "Knapton et al.28 reported that the highly selective detection of CW agent mimics can be achieved by judicious combination of carefully designed fluorescent ligands and metal ions. Designed sensor arrays of these multi-metal and -ligand systems represent a modular and versatile approach for the detection of organophosphates and other analytes."

BODY-24   "In 2012, Lee, Seo, and Kim31 reported a colorimetric method of detecting chloro and fluorophosphates using a dye that was built around polydiacetylene (PDA). The PDA was modified by incorporation of OX functional groups, which were then self-assembled in aqueous solution to form OX–PDA liposomes. The resulting functionalized polymer exhibited a distinct color change, from blue to pink, upon exposure to DCP and DFP. Adding to its potential flexibility as a colorimetric indicator, the polymer was tested in the forms of an aqueous solution, a gel, and a solid on a membrane …"

BODY-25   "As shown in Figure 17, exposure to DCNP generates irreversible cyclization (part a; red bracket on the left) to produce a morpholino cation, while exposure to visible light generates reversible cyclization at the triene (part b; red bracket on the right) to yield a zwitterionic cyclopentenone form. In both cases, the result is a loss of the 550 nm absorption band and bleaching of the dye."

BODY-26   "Enzymes can show very high levels of selectivity due to the 'lock and key' nature of the enzyme active sites and inhibitors. When acetylcholinesterase (AChE) is used as the enzyme, an inhibitor that binds to it is highly likely to show a nerve-agent response in humans. Emerging threat compounds that exhibit nerve-agent activity can be detected in this way, without the need to know the actual structure of the nerve agent. The enzymes also can show exceptional sensitivity."

BODY-27   "There has been an explosion in research to identify colorimetric and enzyme-based indicators that will detect nerve agents in a practical, quick, and easy manner. Dozens of colorimetric indicators have been developed that show promise with nerve-agent mimics. We have not found reports of indicators that have been tested against actual agents. However, it will be interesting to learn whether work with mimics has guided at least some of the indicator development in the right direction, *or whether significant modification of the indicators is necessary to achieve good results with actual agents."*

U.S. ARMY COMBAT CAPABILITIES DEVELOPMENT COMMAND
CHEMICAL BIOLOGICAL CENTER

ABERDEEN PROVING GROUND, MD 21010-5424

CCDC CBC-TR-1576

Literature Review of Colorimetric Indicators for Nerve-Agent Detection

H. Dupont Durst
David J. McGarvey
Alan C. Samuels
RESEARCH AND TECHNOLOGY DIRECTORATE

Barry R. Williams
LEIDOS, INC.
Abingdon, MD 21009-1261

February 2023

Disclaimer

The findings of this report are not to be construed as an official Department of the Army position unless so designated by other authorizing documents.

REPORT DOCUMENTATION PAGE

1. REPORT DATE	2. REPORT TYPE		3. DATES COVERED		
XX-02-2023	Final		**START DATE** Jan 2015		**END DATE** Jun 2017

4. TITLE AND SUBTITLE
Literature Review of Colorimetric Indicators for Nerve-Agent Detection

5a. CONTRACT NUMBER	5b. GRANT NUMBER	5c. PROGRAM ELEMENT NUMBER

5d. PROJECT NUMBER	5e. TASK NUMBER	5f. WORK UNIT NUMBER

6. AUTHOR(S)
Durst, H. Dupont; McGarvey, David J.; Samuels, Alan C. (DEVCOM CBC); and Williams, Barry R. (Leidos)

7. PERFORMING ORGANIZATION NAME(S) AND ADDRESS(ES)	8. PERFORMING ORGANIZATION REPORT NUMBER
U.S. Army Combat Capabilities Development Command Chemical Biological Center; 8198 Blackhawk Road, Aberdeen Proving Ground, MD 21010-5424	CCDC CBC-TR-1576

9. SPONSORING/MONITORING AGENCY NAME(S) AND ADDRESS(ES)	10. SPONSOR/MONITOR'S ACRONYM(S)	11. SPONSOR/MONITOR'S REPORT NUMBER(S)
Defense Threat Reduction Agency, Joint Science and Technology Office; 5801 Telegraph Road, Alexandria, VA 22310-3398	DTRA JSTO	

12. DISTRIBUTION/AVAILABILITY STATEMENT
Approved for public release: distribution unlimited.

13. SUPPLEMENTARY NOTES
U.S. Army Combat Capabilities Development Command Chemical Biological Center (DEVCOM CBC) was previously known as U.S. Army Edgewood Chemical Biological Center (ECBC).
Authors H. Dupont Durst and Barry R. Williams have retired and are no longer affiliated with DEVCOM CBC and Leidos, respectively.

14. ABSTRACT (LESS THAN 200 WORDS)
This technical report is a review of published scientific literature regarding the development and use of colorimetric and fluorescent indicators as a means of detecting nerve agents.

15. SUBJECT TERMS

Nerve agent	Detection	Fluorescence
Indicators	Colorimetric	

16. SECURITY CLASSIFICATION OF:			17. LIMITATION OF ABSTRACT	18. NUMBER OF PAGES
a. REPORT	b. ABSTRACT	C. THIS PAGE		
U	U	U	UU	36

19a. NAME OF RESPONSIBLE PERSON	19b. PHONE NUMBER (Include area code)
Renu B. Rastogi	(410) 436-7545

STANDARD FORM 298 (REV. 5/2020)
Prescribed by ANSI Std. Z39.18

Blank

PREFACE

The work described in this report was started in January 2015 and completed in June 2017. At the time this work was performed, the U.S. Army Combat Capabilities Development Command Chemical Biological Center (DEVCOM CBC; Aberdeen Proving Ground, MD) was known as the U.S. Army Edgewood Chemical Biological Center (ECBC).

The use of either trade or manufacturers' names in this report does not constitute an official endorsement of any commercial products. This report may not be cited for purposes of advertisement.

This report has been approved for public release.

Blank

CONTENTS

FIGURES

LITERATURE REVIEW OF COLORIMETRIC INDICATORS FOR NERVE-AGENT DETECTION

1.   INTRODUCTION

Modern chemical analysis systems can provide volumes of structural information, often at previously unimaginably low limits of detection. Some of these instruments have been ruggedized for use in the field. Notwithstanding the availability of such sophisticated detection instruments, classic and simple colorimetric indicators still offer an easy and quick method to screen for the presence or absence of nerve-agent material. As a low-cost screening method, colorimetric indicators require minimal user training. In use, they yield rapidly acquired information that can be supplemented with additional instrumental analysis in the event of a positive colorimetric response.

2.   COLORIMETRIC INDICATORS

2.1   Fluorophosphate Detection of G-Analog Nerve Agents

A potential problem with using colorimetric indicators to detect nerve agents is that false-positive results may occur when a non-chemical warfare (CW) material triggers a color change. In 2011, Gotor et al.[1] reported the first example of a molecule that reduces the possibility of a false positive by using a two-step process to trigger the color change (Figure 1). In the first step, the alcohol functional group nucleophilically attacks the phosphorus center of a fluorophosphate, causing the release of fluoride ions. An elimination reaction forms a more highly conjugated system, and the color changes to green (from the original clear solution). In a second step, the fluoride ions may react with the silicon atom of the *tert*-butyldimethylsilyl (TBDMS) group. Releasing that group forms a ketone and produces a pink color. Because most common nucleophiles do not react with silicon in this way, significant selectivity is gained by this additional step.

This reaction series with the fluorophosphate compound could indicate that a similar reaction would occur with the fluorophosphonates sarin (isopropyl methylphosphonofluoridate; GB) and soman (pinacolyl methylphosphonofluoridate; GD), or that a molecule similar to this colorimetric probe could be designed to work with GB and GD.

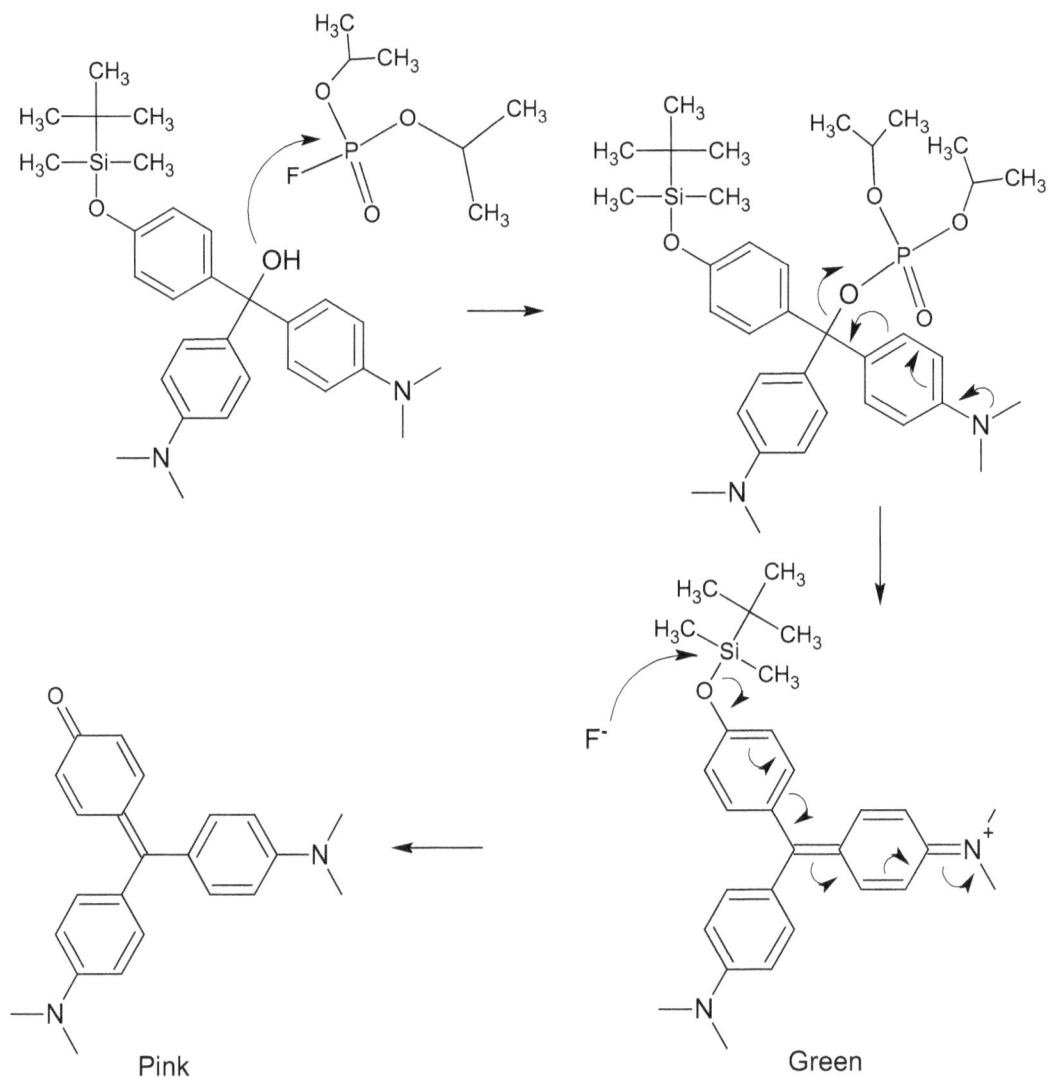

Figure 1. Reaction pathway for Gil's two-step indicator.[1]

The researchers also used a tabun (*O*-ethyl-*N,N*-dimethyl phosphoramidocyanidate; GA) simulant, diethyl cyanophosphonate (DCNP, Figure 2) to show that, as expected, the cyano leaving group from the initial reaction with the indicator was incapable of removing the TBDMS group, and the solution remained green.

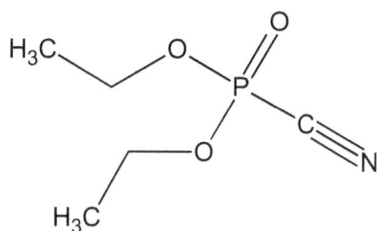

Figure 2. DCNP.

In 2014, El Sayed et al.[2] reported an improved colorimetric indicator (Figure 3) involving diisopropyl fluorophosphate (DFP). This molecule also features a two-step reaction pathway that is similar to the mechanism shown in Figure 1.

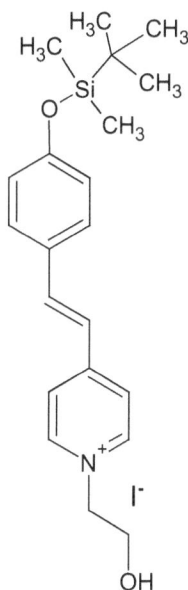

Figure 3. Colorimetric indicator for DFP.

This molecular probe shows activity in solution at a 99:1 solvent-to-DFP ratio, and it also shows activity when challenged with gas-phase DFP. Eight different organophosphorus (OP) compounds of lower toxicity were tested, and none of them caused the diagnostic color change. Fluoride ions exhibited a lower but noticeable color change in the probe. Test strips embedded with this compound were developed and tested. Good selectivity was shown when DFP and DCNP were compared. An approximate concentration could be determined over the test range by just looking at the color intensity. This molecule shows great promise as a potential detector for fluorine-containing OP compounds such as sarin and soman; or, depending on test results with actual agents, it may provide a good lead compound that can be optimized for these agents.

2.2   Cyanophosphate Detection of Tabun and Related Compounds

In 2011, Royo et al.[3] published the first example of a tabun-specific colorimetric indicator. They synthesized the compound shown in Figure 4 (left), which reacts nucleophilically with DCNP to produce the middle compound, which was not isolated. The second step was surprising to the researchers as well as these authors. Although they expected to see a nucleophilic attack at one of the pyridine carbons or possibly at the azo linkage between the aromatic rings, the actual product was the one shown, in which the phosphate group has relocated to the aniline ring. The driving force for this reaction is not clear. It could be caused by the sterically less-hindered pyridine reaction taking place (for kinetic reasons), which would be irreversible for the non-cyanide-containing phosphates. Having the better nucleophile cyanide present (as compared to chloride or fluoride) may allow this reaction to be reversible, and it may also allow for the more thermodynamically stable quaternary amine product to be favored over time.

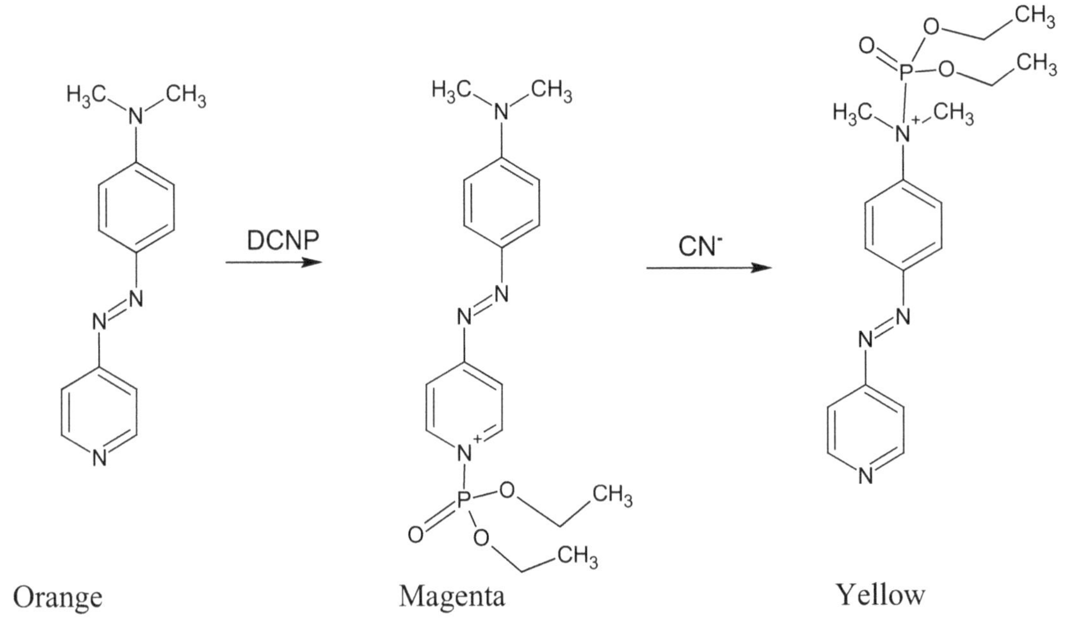

Orange   Magenta   Yellow

Figure 4. Reaction pathway for relocation of DCNP.

The structure of the final compound was confirmed through spectroscopic evidence as well as control experiments in which cyanide was added to solutions of the magenta compound created with diethyl chlorophosphate (DCP) to show that the presence of cyanide would drive the reaction to the quaternary amine.

In 2014, Goud et al.[4] reported on an indicator that differentiates the tabun simulant DCNP from other OP compounds. Figure 5 shows the structure of the probe. The color changes from yellow to blue-green after the addition of as little as 3 mM DCNP. The reaction pathway with DCNP is a two-step process: first, the nucleophilic attack on phosphorus releases cyanide (and incidentally opens the lactam ring); and second, the cyanide undergoes the cyanohydrin reaction with the aldehyde functional group. OP compounds that lack a cyanide leaving group (such as DCP) can undergo this first step to form the red compound shown in Figure 5 (right). Thus, this probe can selectively detect the tabun mimic, and it can also show a different color change for other potentially toxic OP compounds.

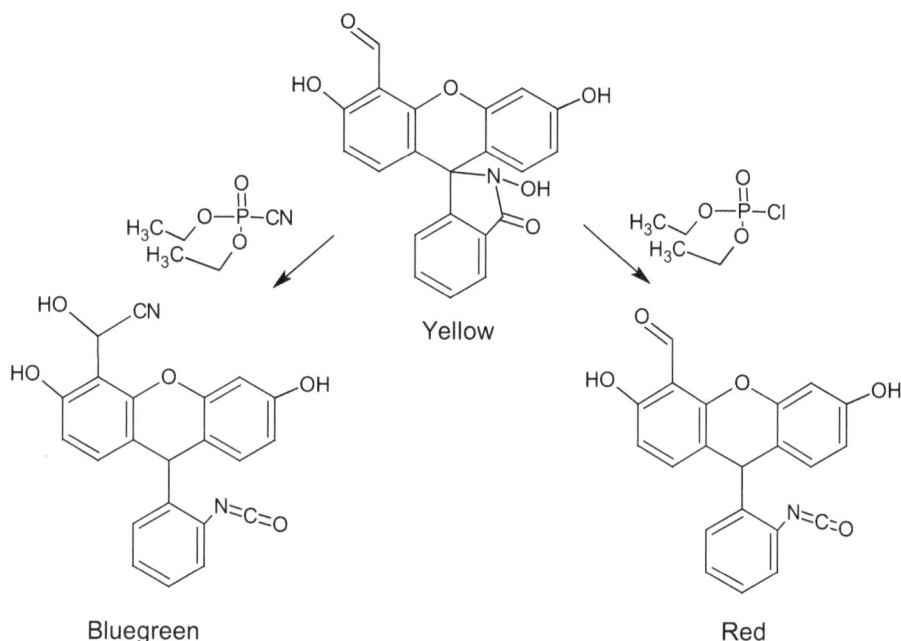

Figure 5. Lactam ring opening and cyanohydrin formation to detect DCNP.

2.3 Colorimetric Indicators with Decontamination Ability

Dale and Rebek[5] produced new nerve-agent sensors that are based on the reaction of β-hydroxy oximes (OXs) with OP agent mimics. The initial reaction induced a cyclization to an (aryl)isoxazole and displacement of the formed OX–OP group to produce noticeable, easily monitored optical changes. A series of sensors built on aromatic cores was synthesized, including more practical water-soluble ones. As compared with previously reported sensors, considerable reaction rate enhancements with OP mimics and greatly increased sensitivity were achieved. Additionally, any detected nerve agent was detoxified upon reaction, thereby creating the potential for the construction of hybrid materials that not only detect the toxins but also simultaneously decompose them.

2.4 Phosphorescent Detection

Heavy-metal complexes that are phosphorescent at room temperature are becoming increasingly important in materials chemistry, principally because of their use in phosphorescent organic light-emitting devices. However, their application in optical sensory schemes has not been heavily explored. Homoleptic bis-cyclometalated Pt(II) complexes are known to undergo oxidative addition with appropriate electrophiles (principally alkyl halides) by either thermal or photochemical activation. Thomas et al.[6] applied this general reaction scheme to the development of a phosphorescence-based sensing system for cyanogen halides. To carry out structure–property relation studies, previously unreported Pt(II) complexes were prepared. Most of the complexes (excluding those that incorporated substituents on the ligands that forced steric crowding in the square plane) were strongly orange-red phosphorescent (fluorescence quantum yield [Φ] of 0.2–0.3) in a room-temperature, oxygen-free solution. These sterically demanding ligands also accelerated the addition of cyanogen bromide (BrCN) to these complexes but slowed the addition of methyl iodide, which indicated that the oxidative addition mechanisms for these two electrophiles were different. The lack of solvent-polarity effect on the addition of BrCN suggests a radical mechanism. Oxidative addition of BrCN to the metal complexes in solution or dispersed in poly(methylmethacrylate) produced blue-shifted emissive Pt(IV) complexes. The blue-shifted products gave a dark-field sensing scheme that contrasted sharply with energy transfer-based sensing schemes. The latter have limited signal-to-noise ratios because the lower-energy vibronic bands of the energy donor can overlap with the emission of the acceptor.

2.5   Fluorescence Detection

A new selective method was developed for the rapid detection of volatile phosphate esters.[7] An immobilized heterocyclic-substituted platinum 1,2-enedithiolate with an appended alcohol was used as the sensor molecule. The volatile fluoro- and cyanoesters were chosen for this study because they are suitable mimics for the three CW agents sarin, soman, and tabun. The new platinum 1,2-enedithiolate complex with an appended alcohol was converted to a room-temperature lumiphore upon exposure to selected phosphate esters (Figure 6).

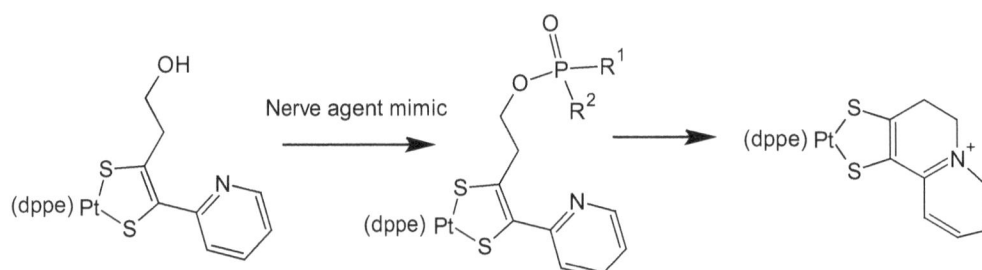

Figure 6. Ring-closing reaction on the platinum heterocycle, where
dppe is 1,2-bis(diphenylphosphino)ethane.

Boron dipyrromethene (BODIPY) forms the framework for a class of fluorescent dyes that has exhibited exponential growth since the 1980s because of the dyes' flexibility, high absorptivity, and generally good quantum yield.[8,9] The most common variant, 4,4-difluoro-4-borata-3a-azonia-4a-aza-s-indacene, is fluorinated (Figure 7) and is sometimes abbreviated F-BODIPY.[9] Because further discussions in this report are limited to derivatives of only the fluorinated form shown in Figure 7, the shorthand abbreviation, BODIPY, is used herein.

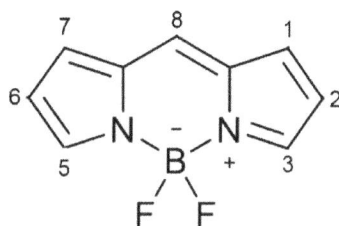

Figure 7. Framework of BODIPY dye and its numbering scheme. Positions 3 and 5 may also be called α; positions 1, 2, 6, and 7 are β; and position 8 is *meso*.[8] The structure shown, 4,4-difluoro-4-borata-3a-azonia-4a-aza-*s*-indacene, is the most common variant and is also abbreviated as F-BODIPY.[9]

Despite the popularity of BODIPY dyes in the peer-reviewed literature, their potential use for detection and identification of CW agents was largely unexplored until relatively recently. In 2014, Barba-Bon et al.[10] reported the use of two BODIPY dyes as potential fluorescent and colorimetric indicators. A problem with some indicators is that they may yield a false-positive result when exposed to an acid.[10] The two BODIPY dyes that were studied were formulated with basic nitrogen (pyridinyl) groups in the molecules and were reported to be less prone to this potential interference. Both dyes exhibited very strong absorption in the visible spectrum and strong fluorescence. Figure 8 shows the variant that exhibited the lowest detection limits for the nerve-agent simulants in acetonitrile solution: DCNP (0.1 ppm) and DFP (0.39 ppm).

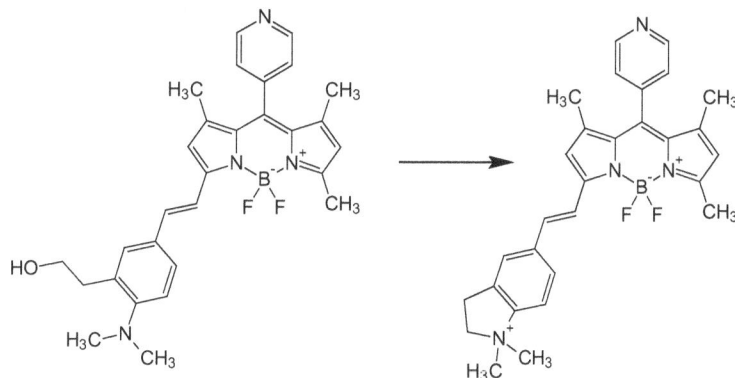

Figure 8. Reaction of a BODIPY dye in response to exposure to a nerve-agent simulant.

Gotor et al.[11] synthesized the BODIPY indicators shown in Figure 9. Two off–on fluorescent chemodosimeters, each based on a BODIPY core, were synthesized for the detection of nerve-agent mimics. They reportedly reacted in a cyclization process that is analogous to that of the previously discussed BODIPY indicators. Their reactivity toward DCNP and DFP was tested in organic and aqueous solutions and in the gas phase. These chemodosimeters selectively detected the nerve-agent mimics with very good limits of detection; many were less than 50 ppm in solution, and for DCNP, only 5 ppm in the vapor phase. The indicators held their sensing properties on solid supports, allowing for the preparation of a handheld sensing kit. The X-ray structure of the second compound was resolved, thereby providing structural confirmation of the indicator as well as detailed information about the fluorophore in the solid state.

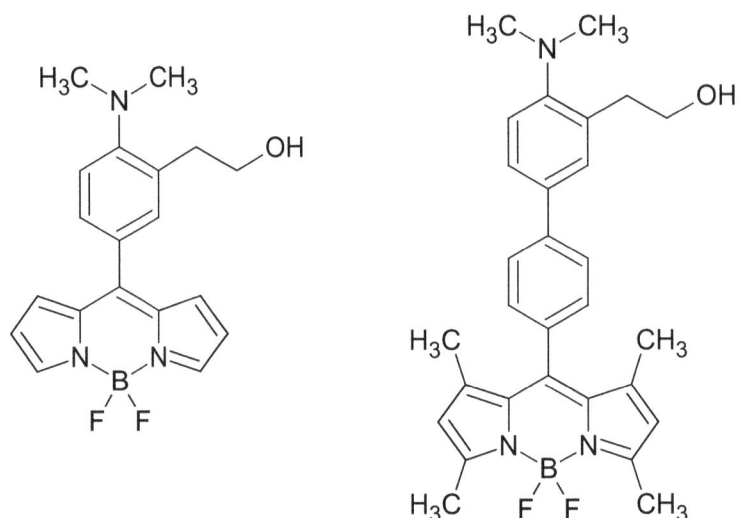

Figure 9. Additional BODIPY dyes for detection of nerve-agent simulants.

Subsequent research on BODIPY dyes by a group of collaborators from Spain, Germany, and the Czech Republic was focused on improving the sensitivity of the dyes and the anchoring of the dyes on supports (for the fabrication of robust tickets for agents in vapor and liquid states). The resulting detector tickets were tested with chemical agents rather than nerve-agent mimics. In 2016 and 2017, Climent et al. reported that they had covalently bound BODIPY at an α-position to a mesoporous silica (SBA) functionalized with (aminopropyl)triethoxysilane (APTES) and had tested for responses to mimics and nerve agents in vapor[12] and in water.[13] The dyes all shared a trimethylphenyl at the *meso* position but had different functional groups at the remaining α positions.

In these reports,[12,13] the authors detailed SBA-BODIPY performance with 2-phenyl-2-ethanolpyrrolidine, which was attached to the BODIPY through the pyrrolidine nitrogen. For vapor tests, strips were made by spotting SBA-BODIPY onto commercial silica or nitrocellulose strips. Upon exposure to vapor from DCP, DFP, GA, GB, or GD, both the mimics and the nerve agents reacted irreversibly with the ethanol on the pyrrolidine to form a bicyclic molecule that quenched fluorescence when illuminated at 365 nm. Measurable quenching was observed after only 5 s of exposure in the microgram-per-cubic-meter range for the mimics and for GA, GB, and GD. Curiously, the dye performance was reported to be slightly better for the mimics than for the nerve agents. A suspension of dye in water was used to test the mimics and the nerve agents. At mimic or agent concentrations of 180 μM, the half-life for the reaction with SBA-BODIPY ranged from 2.67 s (for DFP) to 34.66 s (for GB). Limits of detection for DFP, DCNP, and DCP were found to be 0.12, 16.9, and 90.8 pM, respectively. Structures of BODIPY and the bicyclic reaction product with the nerve agents and mimics, along with SBA-BODIPY, are shown in Figure 10.

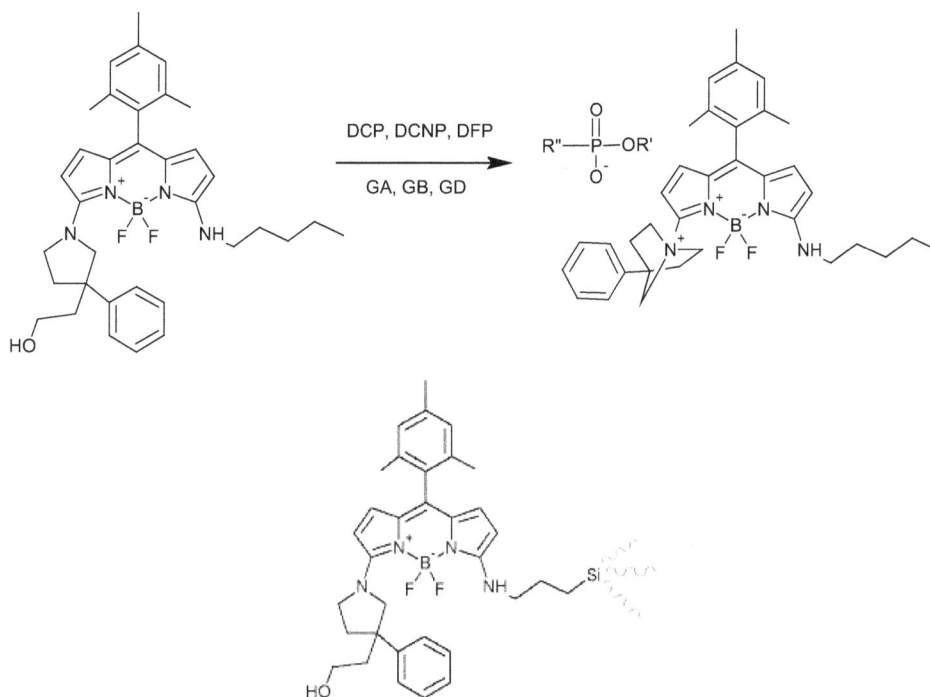

Figure 10. Functionalized BODIPY that was reported in 2016 and 2017 to react with nerve agents and nerve-agent mimics in vapor[12] and water.[13] (Top) BODIPY structure and bicyclic product of its reaction with agents and mimics. (Bottom) Anchored BODIPY formed by covalent bonding to silica through SBA-APTES.

Goswami et al.[14] have published research on rhodamine-based dyes as fluorometric indicators for nerve agents. The unique spirolactam derivative of rhodamine has been dubbed RHM by the researchers and is shown in Figure 11. DCP reacts with this indicator in two steps: first, a nucleophilic attack by the amine on the phosphorus center of DCP; and second, a ring closing (and opening) reaction to form the compound on the right.

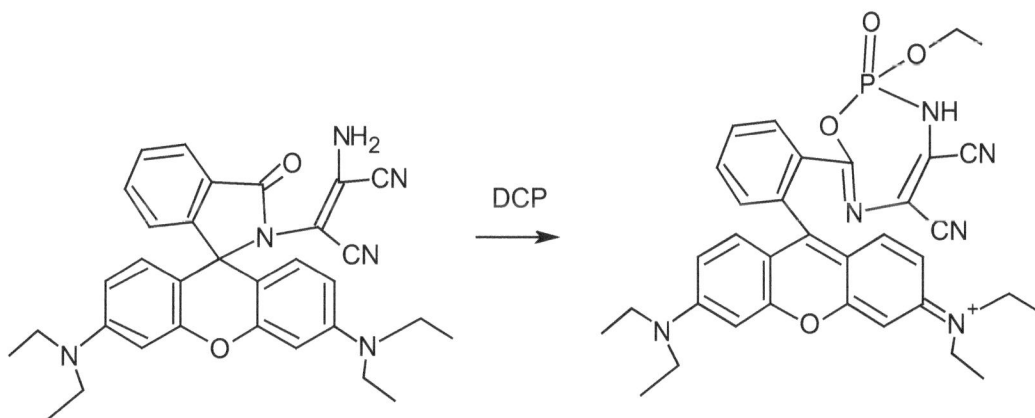

Figure 11. Reaction of the rhodamine-based dye with DCP.

This somewhat complex chemical reaction takes place in less than 8 min. A distinct pink color was observed for DCP, but not for any of the other 12 potential interferents they tested, including dimethyl methylphosphonate (DMMP), metal ions, bleach, and hydrogen peroxide. This indicator also worked well in vapor-phase experiments.

Lei and Yang[15] researched a new fluorescent indicator (Figure 12) that uses a phenylogous Vilsmeier–Haack reaction to initiate a ring-closing reaction, which produces a colored and highly fluorescent product. Modifying the Vilsmeier–Haack reaction in this way was an innovative approach to producing a chromophore that is capable of fluorescence. The indicator is colorless and does not fluoresce, thereby providing a zero background for the analysis. The molecule is small and relatively easy to produce. In a solution of as little as 50 mM (in a series of different solvents), the final solution was a visible light pink color, and it fluoresced strongly when excited by a 532 nm laser.

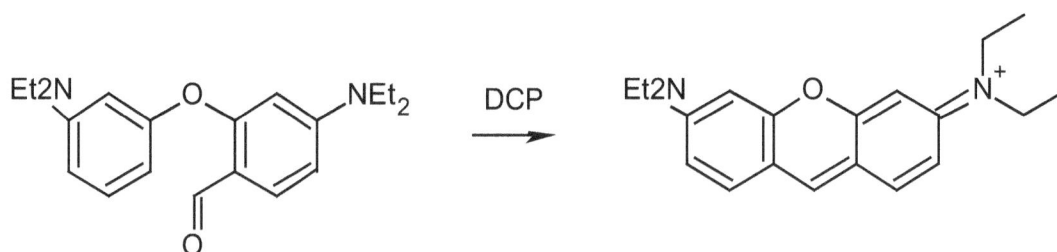

Figure 12. Vilsmeier–Haack ring-closing reaction.

Rusu et al.[16] approached this detection problem by attaching a reactive fluorometric group to a polysiloxane "smart" polymer (structure is shown in Figure 13). The phenolic group can react with an electrophile, such as DCP, and the corresponding adduct shows a change in its fluorescent emission. The sensitivity is quite remarkable: positive detection is possible at 12 ppb.

Because the reaction with DCP produces HCl as a byproduct, Rusu et al. investigated the effect of HCl in a series of control experiments. Dynamic light scattering (DLS) experiments were conducted to investigate nanoscale changes in polymer materials during the reaction. Reaction with DCP appeared to increase hydrophobicity and lead to cluster formation and, eventually, precipitation of the polymer system. Thus, the DLS experiments present another method for confirming the presence of a chemical agent simulant. Additionally, it may be possible to use this change in hydrophobicity and subsequent change in state to create wearable fabrics that can perform both detection and protection.

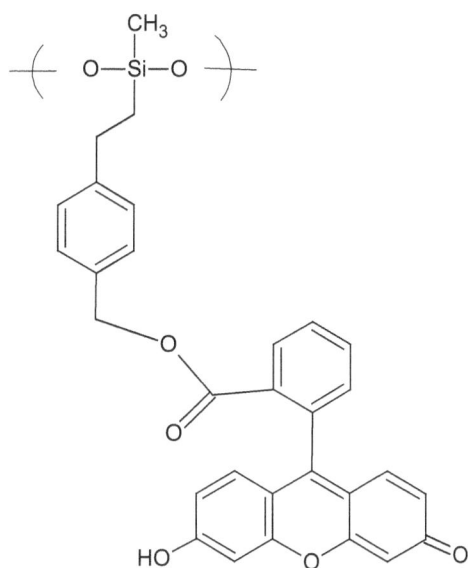

Figure 13. A polysiloxane "smart" material with a fluorescent dye.

Xuan et al.[17] presented a new ratiometric fluorescent probe (Figure 14) that responds to DCP in less than 1 min at concentrations as low as 0.17 ppm. Color changes can also be seen under UV light or with the naked eye. This was the second fluorescent probe system to use Förster resonance energy transfer (FRET) in a ratiometric probe. FRET involves the transfer of energy from one chromophore to another through nonradiative dipole–dipole coupling. This probe responded to both vapor- and solution-phase agent simulants.

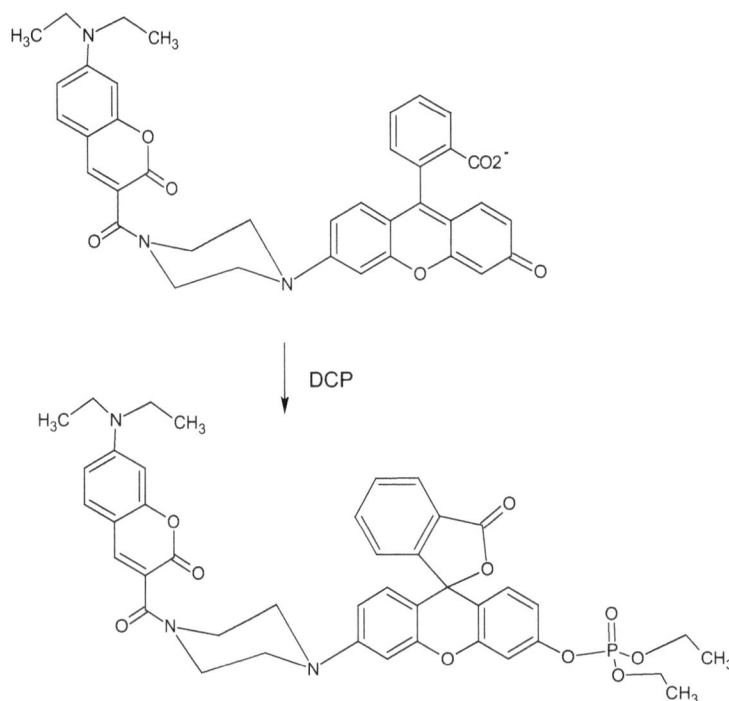

Figure 14. Fluorescent probe using FRET.

Hamel et al.[18] studied fluorescein and resorufin (Figure 15, left and right, respectively), as well as the sodium salts of these compounds. They observed that in a few seconds, a turn-off fluorescence response of the sensor could be seen for parts-per-billion levels of DCP. For instance, fluorescent quenching, $I/I_0 = 0.68$ (where I is the intensity after the quenching process and I_0 is the initial intensity), was obtained when the sensor was exposed to 16 ppb of DCP.

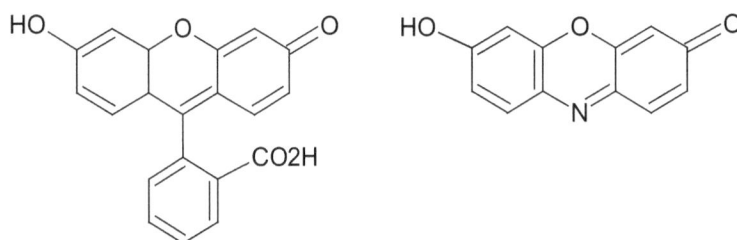

Figure 15. Fluorescein (left) and resorufin (right) fluorescent indicators.

Several possible interferent molecules were studied, including DMMP, tributyl phosphate, and the pesticide dichlorvos. Resorufin showed a small fluorescent response when higher concentrations of dichlorvos were introduced; but otherwise, little interference was observed. The researchers showed that vapor-phase detection was also very sensitive, and that DCP could be detected at its vapor pressure. This system could provide real-time monitoring, given that response times as short as 3 s were observed. The authors indicated that testing with sarin would be undertaken in the future.

Fluorescent microspheres of polystyrene-based Eu(III) complexes were prepared from TentaGel resin (Rapp Polymere GmbH; Tuebingen, Germany), 2,6-bis(benzimidazolyl)pyridine, and europium nitrate.[19] The microspheres were characterized by Fourier transform infrared spectroscopy, elemental analysis, X-ray photoelectron spectroscopy, and fluorescence spectroscopy. Characteristic red emission under irradiation by 365 nm light from a handheld UV lamp was observed for the microspheres in solution and in a solid state. Fluorescent quenching was observed when the microspheres were exposed to a trace amount of DCP in the dispersion. The material and property can potentially be used to fabricate a chemosensor for detection of organophosphates.

N-(rhodamine B)-deoxylactam-5-amino-1-pentanol was designed and prepared as a chromofluorogenic sensor for the detection of a nerve-agent simulant via analyte-triggered tandem phosphorylation and opening of the intramolecular deoxylactam.[20] The successful detection of DCP suggested the utility of rhodamine deoxylactams as a chromofluorogenic signal-reporting platform for the design of sensors to target reactive chemical species via various chemistries.

Azab et al.[21] described the application of time-resolved fluorescence in microtiter plates and electrochemical methods on glassy carbon electrodes for investigating the interactions of europium-3-carboxycoumarin with pesticides aldicarb, methomyl, and prometryne. Stern–Volmer studies at different temperatures indicated that static quenching dominated for methomyl, aldicarb, and prometryne. By applying the Lineweaver–Burk equation, binding constants were detected at 303, 308, and 313 K. A thermodynamic analysis showed that the reaction was spontaneous, with the change in Gibbs free energy (ΔG) being negative. The enthalpy (ΔH) and entropy (ΣS) of the reactions were all determined. A time-resolved (gated) luminescence-based method for the detection of pesticides in microtiter plate format using the long-lived europium-3-carboxycoumarin was developed. The limits of detection were 4.80, 5.06, and 8.01 μmol L^{-1} for methomyl, prometryne, and aldicarb, respectively. This was reported to be the lowest limit of detection achieved thus far for luminescent lanthanide-based pesticide probes. The interaction of the probe with the pesticides was investigated using cyclic voltammetry (CV), differential pulse polarography, square-wave voltammetry (SWV), and linear sweep voltammetry (LSV) on a glassy carbon electrode using 0.1 mol L^{-1} *p*-toluenesulfonate as the supporting electrolyte at 25 °C. The diffusion coefficients of the reduced species were calculated. The main properties of the electrode reaction occurring in a finite diffusion space were the quasi-reversible maximum and the splitting of the net SWV peak for Eu(III) ions in the ternary complex that was formed. The increase of the cathodic peak current using LSV was linear with the increase of pesticide concentration, in the range of 5 × 10^{-7} to 1 × 10^{-5} mol L^{-1}. The limits of detection were about 1.01, 2.23, and 1.89 μmol L^{-1} for aldicarb, methomyl, and prometryne, respectively. To assess the analytical applicability of the method, the influence of various potentially interfering species was examined. Specifically, the influence of interfering species on the recovery of 10 μmol L^{-1} pesticides was investigated.

Candel et al.[22] reported a hybrid, nanoscopic, capped mesoporous material that is selectively opened in the presence of nerve-agent simulants. It was prepared and used as a probe for the chromofluorogenic detection of these chemicals. A mesoporous alumosilicate material, MCM-41 (Mobil Composition of Matter No. 41), was prepared as the scaffolding on which tris(2,2'-bipyridyl)ruthenium(II) chloride dye was loaded. MCM-41 was capped with bis(2-hydroxyethyl)aminopropyltriethoxysilane, which reacted with nerve-agent simulant DCP to release the dye and thereby indicate its presence in a chromogenic response.

Kim et al.[23] synthesized a monopyrene-imine derivative that is a highly selective and sensitive "turn-on" fluorogenic probe for DCP. Upon addition of DCP to a solution of this probe, a phosphoramidate was formed that exhibited an enhanced fluorescence emission at 425 nm. When exposed to DCP in the vapor phase, the indicator impregnated on silica gel showed a sky-blue fluorescence.

Han et al.[24] devised a visual and fluorogenic detection method for a nerve-agent simulant that was based on a Lossen rearrangement of rhodamine–hydroxamate in the presence of DCP under alkaline conditions.

Climent et al.[25] developed an approach for the chromogenic sensing of nerve-agent mimics by using silica nanoparticles (SNPs) that were functionalized with aliphatic alcohol and thiol moieties. When a solution of squaraine dye (SD) was added to a suspension of the functionalized SNPs, the reaction between the thiol moieties and the squaraine caused bleaching of the blue dye. However, when nerve-agent mimics were added to the hybrid SNP suspensions, the OP reacted with the hydroxyl groups of the alcohol moieties. This hindered the access of SD to the thiols of the SNPs, and the solutions remained blue. Several SNP variants were tested, and DFP detection was achieved in concentrations as low as 5×10^{-7} M in mixed solutions containing up to 50% water in acetonitrile. Prototype dipsticks were also prepared by applying the SNPs to a polyethylene terephthalate film that was then used to detect DFP in the vapor phase by dipping the test strips in SD solutions. When the test strips were dipped in the dye, the solution remained blue if the strip had been exposed to DFP, or it became bleached if the strip had not been exposed to DFP.

Costero et al.[26] designed and synthesized a family of azo and stilbene derivatives and investigated their chromofluorogenic behavior in the presence of nerve-agent simulants DCP, DFP, and DCNP in acetonitrile and mixed water/acetonitrile solutions (3:1 v/v) buffered at pH 5.6 with 2-(N-morpholino)ethanesulfonic acid. The compounds that were prepared contained 2-(2-N,N-dimethylaminophenyl)ethanol or 2-[(2-N,N-dimethylamino)phenoxy]ethanol reactive groups, which are part of the conjugated π system of the dyes and produce acylation reactions with phosphonate substrates followed by rapid intramolecular N-alkylation. The mimic-triggered cyclization reaction transformed a dimethylamino group into a quaternary ammonium. This induced a change in the electronic properties of the delocalized systems that resulted in a hypsochromic shift of the absorption band of the dyes.

Similar reactivity studies were also carried out with other "nontoxic" OP compounds, but no changes in the UV–visible spectra were observed. The emission behavior of the reagents in acetonitrile and water–acetonitrile mixtures (3:1 v/v) was also studied in the presence of nerve-agent simulants and other OP derivatives. The reactivity between the indicators and DCP, DCNP, or DFP in 3:1 v/v buffered water–acetonitrile solutions under pseudo-first-order kinetic conditions, using an excess of the corresponding simulant, were studied to determine the rate constants (k) and the half-life times, $t_{1/2} = \left(\frac{\ln 2}{k} \right)$, for the reactions.

The limits of detection in 3:1 v/v water–acetonitrile were also determined for each indicator and DCP, DCNP, and DFP. Finally, the chromogenic detection of nerve-agent simulants in solution and in the gas phase were tested using silica gel-containing adsorbed indicators with fine results.

Costero et al.[27] presented a new chromogenic protocol for the selective detection of nerve-agent mimics. This indicator (Figure 16) showed selective reactivity with three nerve-agent simulants and did not respond to a variety of tested interferent molecules.

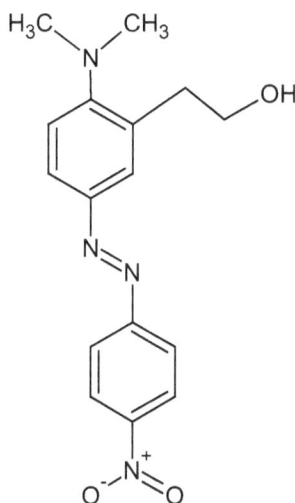

Figure 16. Costero et al.'s fluorescent indicator.[27]

Knapton et al.[28] reported that the highly selective detection of CW agent mimics can be achieved by judicious combination of carefully designed fluorescent ligands and metal ions. Designed sensor arrays of these multi-metal and -ligand systems represent a modular and versatile approach for the detection of organophosphates and other analytes.

Van Houten et al.[29] reported research on the emissions from the 2-pyridyl- and 2-pyridinium-substituted platinum-1,2-enedithiolate complexes, $L_2Pt\{S_2C_2[2\text{-pyridyl(ium)}](R)\}$, where L is triphenylphosphine (PPh_3), diphenyl methylphosphine (PPh_2Me), phenyl dimethyl phosphine ($PPhMe_2$), and P(propyl)$_3$; and L_2 is dppm, dppe, and dppp. These were studied in DMMP (DMF–CH_2Cl_2–MeOH at a 1:1:1 v/v/v ratio, where DMF is dimethyl formamide and MeOH is methanol) glasses at 77 K. All of the pyridyl-substituted complexes had an emission between 18,600 and 17,900 cm^{-1} with pronounced 1200 cm^{-1} vibronic structure. The lifetimes of the pyridyl-substituted complexes were 216–350 µs. The pyridinium-substituted complexes had emissions in the range of 16,600–16,100 cm^{-1} and had less-resolved vibronic structure than their pyridyl counterparts. The lifetimes of the pyridinium-substituted complexes were 158–290 µs. The emissions at 77 K from the pyridyl- and pyridinium-substituted complexes contrasted with those from the room-temperature studies, where only selected pyridinium complexes were emissive.

Zhang and Swager[30] researched indicators that provide a highly sensitive and functional group-specific fluorescent response to DFP. A nonemissive phenylpyridyl indicator reacted with DFP to yield a cyclized compound that showed high emission due to its highly planar and rigid structure. Very weak emission was observed by the addition of HCl. Another indicator based on pyridyl naphthalene exhibited a large shift in its emission spectrum after reaction with DFP, which provided for quantitative ratiometric detection.

2.6 Synthetic Carbon-Based Polymers for Detection of Nerve Agents

Given their ability to be shaped into a virtually infinite variety of forms with a vast array of physical and chemical properties, organic polymers have formed an essential part of biochemistry since the origins of life and have been a vital branch of synthetic chemistry since the invention of the first artificial plastics in the early 20th century. In the 2010s, several groups of researchers investigated novel avenues to nerve-agent detection using synthetic polymers functionalized with colorimetric and fluorometric sensors.

In 2012, Lee, Seo, and Kim[31] reported a colorimetric method of detecting chloro- and fluorophosphates using a dye that was built around polydiacetylene (PDA). The PDA was modified by incorporation of OX functional groups, which were then self-assembled in aqueous solution to form OX–PDA liposomes. The resulting functionalized polymer exhibited a distinct color change, from blue to pink, upon exposure to DCP and DFP. Adding to its potential flexibility as a colorimetric indicator, the polymer was tested in the forms of an aqueous solution, a gel, and a solid on a membrane, and it responded to the simulants in all three matrices. OX–PDA on cellulose acetate gave a detectable color change to DFP vapor at 160 mg m^{-3} in under 1 min. OX–PDA gave little or no response to HF, HCl, and phosphoric acid. Also of interest, the reaction between OX–PDA and simulants detoxified DCP and DFP, leading to the potential use of the polymer as a decontaminating agent with a built-in indicator.

More recently, Sarkar and Shunmugam[32] reported the use of a norborene-based, triazolyl-functionalized 8-hydroxyquinoline polymer (NCHQ) that upon phosphorylation exhibited an intense fluorescent response through photoinduced electron transfer. In tests with DCP and diphenyl chlorophosphate, the researchers claimed that the material was the first polymeric sensor to show an "instantaneous" response to the simulants at concentrations as low as 25 ppb of DCP in methanol. The simple technique of applying an NCHQ solution to a strip of Whatman filter paper and drying the filter resulted in a detector paper that, under UV illumination and upon exposure to DCP vapor, would exhibit a visible green emission within 1 s.

In 2015, Weis and Swager[33] reported the synthesis of four reactive materials from dithienobenzotropone-based conjugated alternating copolymers that were subjected to hydride reduction to yield reactive hydroxyl groups. The light-yellow-colored polymers reacted at the hydroxyl with both DCP and DFP to form a bright-blue-colored, resonance-stabilized tropylium ion. The incorporation of hydrogel-promoting tetra(ethylene glycol) side chains and subsequent hydride reduction yielded a stable polymer with a number-average molecular weight (M_n) of 16.6 kDa and a limit of detection of 6 ppm for DCP in the vapor phase. Adding to the potential usefulness of the material, the authors reported it was possible to regenerate the reactive hydroxyl groups by treating the DCP vapor-exposed polymer with ammonium hydroxide vapor.

Most recently, Balamurugan and Lee[34] reported the use of a polymer with a donor–acceptor Stenhouse adduct (DASA) that has a somewhat complex response to DCNP. The polymer was synthesized starting with reversible addition–fragmentation chain transfer polymerization to yield poly(glycidyl methacrylate-co-dimethylacrylamide) (P1; where m:n, the ratio of repeating units in the overall polymer, was 6:94). P1 was then further reacted with 2-(2-aminoethoxy)ethanol to give P2. Finally, P2 was reacted with 5-(furan-2-ylmethylene)-1,3-dimethylpyrimidine-2,4,6($1H,3H,5H$)-trione to yield P3. P3 exhibited an on–off colorimetric response to DCNP in the vapor phase and in some organic solvents. Switching of the polymer was also reported to be governed by exposure to visible light. The structure of P3, as well as a simplified explanation of its reactions of the polymer with DCNP and light, are shown in Figure 17.

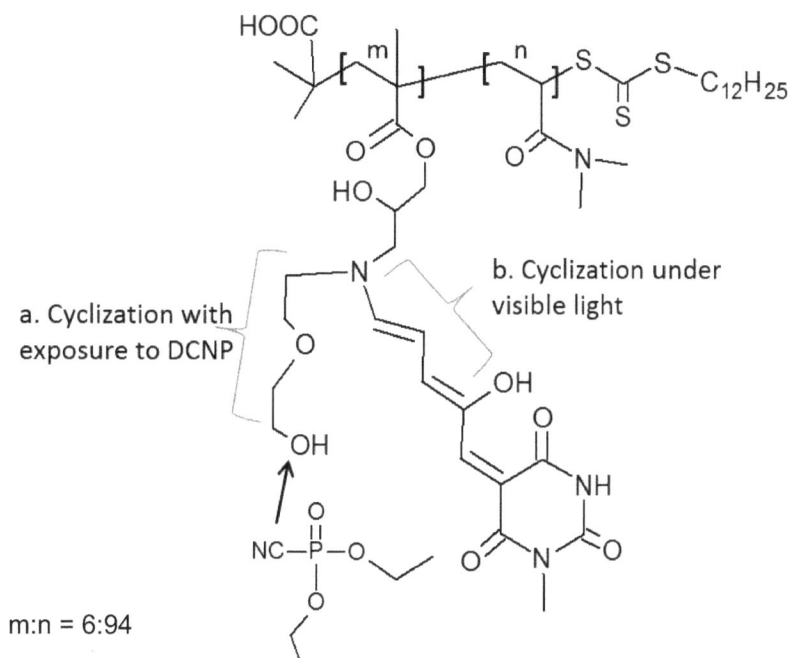

Figure 17. Polymeric probe incorporating a DASA reported by Balamurugan and Lee.[34]

As synthesized, the polymer exhibits a strong absorption near 550 nm, giving it a strong purple color. As shown in Figure 17, exposure to DCNP generates irreversible cyclization (part a; red bracket on the left) to produce a morpholino cation, while exposure to visible light generates reversible cyclization at the triene (part b; red bracket on the right) to yield a zwitterionic cyclopentenone form. In both cases, the result is a loss of the 550 nm absorption band and bleaching of the dye.

3.   ENZYME-BASED INDICATORS

3.1   Background

Enzyme-based systems have several potential advantages over chemical indicators. Enzymes can show very high levels of selectivity due to the "lock and key" nature of the enzyme active sites and inhibitors. When acetylcholinesterase (AChE) is used as the enzyme, an inhibitor that binds to it is highly likely to show a nerve-agent response in humans. Emerging threat compounds that exhibit nerve-agent activity can be detected in this way, without the need to know the actual structure of the nerve agent. The enzymes also can show exceptional sensitivity. Colorimetric indicators may have advantages in cost and stability that would make them more desirable under certain scenarios; however, enzyme-based methods have great potential for inclusion in a simple and effective detection kit.

3.2   Detection Systems

Reports from as early as 1964 outlined the possibility of using AChE enzymes as a component of a nerve-agent detection system.[35] These simple devices were based on the ability of AChE to react with nerve agents and produce protons as a byproduct of the reaction. An acid/base indicator in the enzyme solution caused a color change that indicated a positive result. A double-valve bulb was used to force ambient air through the solution, thereby allowing for vapor detection of agents.

A number of early studies were reported regarding the use of electrochemical detection in combination with enzymes, including one from Porton Down (Wiltshire, UK) entitled *An Investigation into the Use of Immobilised Cholinesterase for the Automatic Detection of Nerve Agents.*[36] In this detection system, the enzyme was covalently bonded to a polymethacrylate resin. This helped reduce the problem of consuming valuable enzyme by producing a system that could operate on a continuous basis. An ongoing reaction in this system was the conversion of thiocholine to choline disulfide. An electrochemical sensor was placed across the material with the immobilized enzyme, and a constant electrochemical potential occurred when nerve agent was not present. When nerve agent was present, the enzyme was inhibited, the ongoing reaction was halted, and a change in the electrochemical potential was recorded. The method could be used to detect nerve-agent vapor in relatively low concentrations of 0.005 mg/m^3 in less than 5 min. Detection of high concentrations (e.g., 10 mg/m^3) could take place in 5–8 s.

Erbeldinger and LeJeune[37] reported the development of a biopolymer-based wipe that has enzymes integrated into the wipe substrate. The wipe begins as a yellow-colored material that then turns red in the presence of a nerve agent or turns green when exposed to a clean surface. The system uses both the butyrylcholinesterase (BChE) and urease enzymes to detect the agent and provide a color change that is intuitive to a user. The two enzymes act in concert to adjust the solution pH. The presence of agent results in inhibition of the BChE enzyme, which allows the pH to rise. In cases where agent is not present, the urease enzyme creates ammonia, which reacts with the BChE enzyme to lower the pH and trigger the green color.

White and Harmon[38] reported on a highly sensitive enzyme-based sensor that requires more expertise to use. Using planar waveguide absorbance spectroscopy, they were able to achieve detection levels of 100 parts per trillion in solution and 250 pg in vapor.

Upadhyay et al.[39] discovered a system for detecting nerve agents by using immobilized enzymes attached to gold–platinum nanoparticles that were deposited onto a 3-aminopropyltriethoxysilane-modified glassy carbon electrode. Electrochemical detection was then used to identify the presence of sarin and several pesticides.

It was also shown that BChE can be used with peptide nanotubes (PNTs) to allow for electrochemical detection (by CV, in this case).[40] The electrochemical signal was produced by the conversion of butyrylthiocholine by the BChE enzyme. As the BChE enzyme is inhibited by a nerve agent, the cyclic voltammogram records the change in voltage. A CV-based system would likely be difficult to field, although the concept of immobilization on the PNTs could be useful in another context.

Researchers at Oklahoma State University (Stillwater, OK) developed a method for using both AChE and BChE to detect the presence of enzyme inhibitors.[41] When tetraphenylporphyrins were added to the system, a colorimetric change occurred. Absorbance of the porphyrins is normally seen at 446 and 421 nm. Loss of absorbance was identified in the system when one of the enzymes was inhibited.

4.   CONCLUSIONS

There has been an explosion in research to identify colorimetric and enzyme-based indicators that will detect nerve agents in a practical, quick, and easy manner. Dozens of colorimetric indicators have been developed that show promise with nerve-agent mimics. We have not found reports of indicators that have been tested against actual agents. However, it will be interesting to learn whether work with mimics has guided at least some of the indicator development in the right direction, or whether significant modification of the indicators is necessary to achieve good results with actual agents.

Enzyme-based systems can show high selectivity and sensitivity toward nerve agents. These systems have been developed into devices that range from simple to complex. Easily used wipes can provide a visible color change in the event of detection. Other systems are designed to use electrochemical or spectroscopic detection, through which more quantitative information about nerve agent concentration might be possible.

Blank

LITERATURE CITED

1. Gotor, R.; Costero, A.M.; Gil, S.; Parra, M.; Martínez-Máñez, R.; Sancenón, F. A Molecular Probe for the Highly Selective Chromogenic Detection of DFP, a Mimic of Sarin and Soman Nerve Agents. *Chemistry* **2011,** *17,* 11994–11997.

2. El Sayed, S.; Pascual, L.; Agostini, A.; Martínez-Máñez, R.; Sancenón, F.; Costero, A.M.; Parra, M.; Gil, S. A Chromogenic Probe for the Selective Recognition of Sarin and Soman Mimic DFP. *ChemistryOpen* **2014,** *3,* 142–145.

3. Royo, S.; Costero, A.M.; Parra, M.; Gil, S.; Martínez-Máñez, R.; Sancenón, F. Chromogenic, Specific Detection of the Nerve-Agent Mimic DCNP (a Tabun Mimic). *Chemistry* **2011,** *17,* 6931–6934.

4. Goud, D.R.; Pardasani, D.; Tak, V.; Dubey, D.K. A Highly Selective Visual Detection of Tabun Mimic Diethyl Cyanophosphate (DCNP): Effective Discrimination of DCNP from Other Nerve Agent Mimics. *RSC Adv.* **2014,** *4,* 24645–24648.

5. Dale, T.J.; Rebek, J., Jr. Hydroxy Oximes as Organophosphorus Nerve Agent Sensors. *Angew. Chem. Int. Ed. Engl.* **2009,** *48,* 7850–7852.

6. Thomas, S.W., III; Venkatesan, K.; Mueller, P.; Swager, T.M. Dark-Field Oxidative Addition-Based Chemosensing: New Bis-Cyclometalated Pt(II) Complexes and Phosphorescent Detection of Cyanogen Halides. *J. Am. Chem. Soc.* **2006,** *128,* 16641–16648.

7. Van Houten, K.A.; Heath, D.C.; Pilato, R.S. Rapid Luminescent Detection of Phosphate Esters in Solution and the Gas Phase Using (dppe)Pt{S_2C_2(2-pyridyl)(CH_2CH_2OH)}. *J. Am. Chem. Soc.* **1998,** *120,* 12359–12360.

8. Loudet, A.; Burgess, K. BODIPY Dyes and Their Derivatives: Syntheses and Spectroscopic Properties. *Chem. Rev.* **2007,** *107,* 4891–4932.

9. Ulrich, G.; Ziessel, R.; Harriman, A. The Chemistry of Fluorescent Bodipy Dyes: Versatility Unsurpassed. *Angew. Chem. Int. Ed. Engl.* **2008,** *47,* 1184–1201.

10. Barba-Bon, A.; Costero, A.M.; Gil, S.; Harriman, A.; Sancenón, F. Highly Selective Detection of Nerve-Agent Simulants with BODIPY Dyes. *Chemistry* **2014,** *20,* 6339–6347.

11. Gotor, R.; Gaviña, P.; Ochando, L.E.; Chulvi, K.; Lorente, A.; Martíncz-Máñez, R.; Costero, A.M. BODIPY Dyes Functionalized with 2-(2-Dimethylaminophenyl)ethanol Moieties as Selective Off–On Fluorescent Chemodosimeters for the Nerve Agent Mimics DCNP and DFP. *RSC Adv.* **2014,** *4,* 15975–15982.

12. Climent, E.; Biyikal, M.; Gawlitza, K.; Dropa, T.; Urban, M.; Costero, A.M.; Martínez-Máñez, R.; Rurack, K. A Rapid and Sensitive Strip-Based Quick Test for Nerve Agents Tabun, Sarin, and Soman Using BODIPY-Modified Silica Materials. *Chemistry* **2016,** *22,* 11138–11142.

13. Climent, E.; Biyikal, M.; Gawlitza, K.; Dropa, T.; Urban, M.; Costero, A.M.; Martínez-Máñez, R.; Rurack, K. Determination of the Chemical Warfare Agents Sarin, Soman and Tabun in Natural Waters Employing Fluorescent Hybrid Silica Materials. *Sens. Actuators B Chem.* **2017**, *246,* 1056–1065; http://dx.doi.org/10.1016/j.snb.2017.02.115 (accessed 17 April 2019).

14. Goswami, S.; Manna, A.; Paul, S. Rapid 'Naked Eye' Response of DCP, a Nerve Agent Simulant: From Molecules to Low-Cost Devices for both Liquid and Vapour Phase Detection. *RSC Adv.* **2014**, *4,* 21984–21988.

15. Lei, Z.; Yang, Y. A Concise Colorimetric and Fluorimetric Probe for Sarin Related Threats Designed via the "Covalent-Assembly" Approach. *J. Am. Chem. Soc.* **2014**, *136,* 6594–6597.

16. Rusu, A.D.; Moleavin, I.A.; Hurduc, N.; Hamel, M.; Rocha, L. Fluorescent Polymeric Aggregates for Selective Response to Sarin Surrogates. *Chem. Commun.* **2014,** *50,* 9965–9968.

17. Xuan, W.; Cao, Y.; Zhou, J.; Wang, W. A FRET-Based Ratiometric Fluorescent and Colorimetric Probe for the Facile Detection of Organophosphonate Nerve Agent Mimic DCP. *Chem. Commun.* **2013,** *49,* 10474–10476.

18. Hamel, M.; Hamoniaux, J.; Rocha, L.; Normand, S. Ppb Detection of Sarin Surrogate in Liquid Solutions. In *Proceedings of SPIE 8710: Chemical, Biological, Radiological, Nuclear, and Explosives (CBRNE) Sensing XIV*, 2013, pp 87100H/1–87100H/7.

19. Zhang, H.; Hua, X.; Tuo, X.; Chen, C.; Wang, X. Polystyrene Microsphere-Based Lanthanide Luminescent Chemosensor for Detection of Organophosphate Pesticides. *J. Rare Earth* **2012,** *30,* 1203–1207.

20. Wu, Z.; Wu, X.; Yang, Y.; Wen, T.-B.; Han, S. A Rhodamine-Deoxylactam Based Sensor for Chromo-Fluorogenic Detection of Nerve Agent Simulant. *Bioorg. Med. Chem. Lett.* **2012,** *22,* 6358–6361.

21. Azab, H.A.; Duerkop, A.; Mogahed, E.M.; Awad, F.K.; Abd El Aal, R.M.; Kamel, R.M. Fluorescence and Electrochemical Sensing of Pesticides Methomyl, Aldicarb and Prometryne by the Luminescent Europium-3-carboxycoumarin Probe. *J. Fluoresc.* **2012,** *22,* 659–676.

22. Candel, I.; Bernardos, A.; Climent, E.; Marcos, M.D.; Martínez-Máñez, R.; Sancenón, F.; Soto, J.; Costero, A.; Gil, S.; Parra, M. Selective Opening of Nanoscopic Capped Mesoporous Inorganic Materials with Nerve Agent Simulants; an Application to Design Chromo-Fluorogenic Probes. *Chem. Commun.* **2011,** *47,* 8313–8315.

23. Kim, H.J.; Jang, S.; Ren, W.X.; Bartsch, R.A.; Sohn, H.; Kim, J.S. Imine-Functionalized, Turn-On Fluorophore for DCP. *Sens. Actuators B Chem.* **2011,** *153,* 266–270.

24. Han, S.; Xue, Z.; Wang, Z.; Wen, T.B. Visual and Fluorogenic Detection of a Nerve Agent Simulant via a Lossen Rearrangement of Rhodamine–Hydroxamate. *Chem. Commun.* **2010,** *46,* 8413–8415.

25. Climent, E.; Martí, A.; Royo, S.; Martínez-Máñez, R.; Marcos, M.D.; Sancenón, F.; Soto, J.; Costero, A.M.; Gil, S.; Parra, M. Chromogenic Detection of Nerve Agent Mimics by Mass Transport Control at the Surface of Bifunctionalized Silica Nanoparticles. *Angew. Chem. Int. Ed. Engl.* **2010,** *49,* 5945–5948, S5945/1–S5945/3.

26. Costero, A.M.; Parra, M.; Gil, S.; Gotor, R.; Mancini, P.M.; Martínez-Máñez, R.; Sancenón, F.; Royo, S. Chromo-Fluorogenic Detection of Nerve-Agent Mimics Using Triggered Cyclization Reactions in Push–Pull Dyes. *Chem. Asian J.* **2010,** *5,* 1573–1585.

27. Costero, A.M.; Gil, S.; Parra, M.; Mancini, P.M.E.; Martínez-Máñez, R.; Sancenón, F.; Royo, S. Chromogenic Detection of Nerve Agent Mimics. *Chem. Commun.* **2008,** *45,* 6002–6004.

28. Knapton, D.; Burnworth, M.; Rowan, S.J.; Weder, C. Fluorescent Organometallic Sensors for the Detection of Chemical-Warfare-Agent Mimics. *Angew. Chem. Int. Ed. Engl.* **2006,** *45,* 5825–5829.

29. Van Houten, K.A.; Blough, N.V.; Pilato, R.S. Low Temperature Emission Spectra of 2-Pyridyl-Substituted Platinum-1,2-enedithiolates. *Inorganica Chim. Acta* **2003,** *353,* 231–237.

30. Zhang, S.-W.; Swager, T.M. Fluorescent Detection of Chemical Warfare Agents: Functional Group Specific Ratiometric Chemosensors. *J. Am. Chem. Soc.* **2003,** *125,* 3420–3421.

31. Lee, J.; Seo, S.; Kim, J. Colorimetric Detection of Warfare Gases by Polydiacetylenes toward Equipment-Free Detection. *Adv. Funct. Mater.* **2012,** *22,* 1632–1638.

32. Sarkar, S.; Shunmugam, R. Polynorbornene Derived 8-Hydroxyquinoline Paper Strips for Ultrasensitive Chemical Nerve Agent Surrogate Sensing. *Chem. Commun.* **2014,** *50,* 8511–8513.

33. Weis, J.G.; Swager, T.M. Thiophene-Fused Tropones as Chemical Warfare Agent-Responsive Building Blocks. *ACS Macro Lett.* **2015,** *4,* 138−142.

34. Balamurugan, A.; Lee, H.A. A Visible Light Responsive On–Off Polymeric Photoswitch for the Colorimetric Detection of Nerve Agent Mimics in Solution and in the Vapor Phase. *Macromolecules* **2016,** *49,* 2568−2574.

35. Zacks, S.I.; Blumberg, J.M. Simple and Inexpensive Anti-Cholinesterase Detectors for Field Use. *Mil. Med.* **1964,** *129,* 1084–1086.

36. Lambert, J.; Olsen, E.J.; Stratford, C.; Williams, G. *An Investigation into the Use of Immobilised Cholinesterase for the Automatic Detection of Nerve Agents*; Technical Paper 57; Chemical Defence Establishment: Porton Down, Wiltshire, U.K., 1971; UNCLASSIFIED Report (AD0595689).

37. Erbeldinger, M.; LeJeune, K. *Nerve Agent Sensing Biopolymer Wipe*; BS-041203-ME; U.S. Army Research Office: Research Triangle Park, NC; 2003; UNCLASSIFIED Report (ADA413535).

38. White, B.J.; Harmon, H.J. Enzyme-Based Detection of Sarin (GB) Using Planar Waveguide Absorbance Spectroscopy. *Sens. Lett.* **2005,** *3,* 36–41.

39. Upadhyay, S.; Rao, G.R.; Sharma, M.K.; Bhattacharya, B.K.; Rao, V.K.; Vijayaraghavan, R. Immobilization of Acetylcholineesterase–Choline Oxidase on a Gold–Platinum Bimetallic Nanoparticles Modified Glassy Carbon Electrode for the Sensitive Detection of Organophosphate Pesticides, Carbamates and Nerve Agents. *Biosens. Bioelectron.* **2009,** *25,* 832–838.

40. Edwards, C.W. *Gas Phase Organophosphate Detection Using Enzymes Encapsulated within Peptide Nanotubes*; AFIT-ENV-14-M-41; Air Force Institute of Technology: Wright-Patterson Air Force Base, OH, 2014; UNCLASSIFIED Report (ADA600120).

41. White, B.J.; Legako, A.J.; Harmon, H.J. Spectrophotometric Detection of Cholinesterase Inhibitors with an Integrated Acetyl-/Butyrylcholinesterase Surface. *Sens. Actuators B Chem.* **2003,** *89,* 107–111.

ACRONYMS AND ABBREVIATIONS

ΔG	Gibbs free energy
ΔH	enthalpy
ΣS	entropy
AChE	acetylcholinesterase
APTES	(aminopropyl)triethoxysilane
BChE	butyrylcholinesterase
BODIPY	boron dipyrromethene
BrCN	cyanogen bromide
CV	cyclic voltammetry
CW	chemical warfare
DASA	donor–acceptor Stenhouse adduct
DCNP	diethyl cyanophosphonate
DCP	diethyl chlorophosphate
DFP	diisopropyl fluorophosphate
DLS	dynamic light scattering
DMMP	dimethyl methylphosphonate
F-BODIPY	4,4-difluoro-4-borata-3a-azonia-4a-aza-*s*-indacene
FRET	Förster resonance energy transfer
GA	*O*-ethyl-*N,N*-dimethyl phosphoramidocyanidate; tabun
GB	isopropyl methylphosphonofluoridate; sarin
GD	pinacolyl methylphosphonofluoridate; soman
LSV	linear sweep voltammetry
m:n	ratio of repeating units in the overall polymer
NCHQ	norbornene-based triazolyl functionalized 8-hydroxyquinoline
OP	organophosphorous
OX	oxime
OX–PDA	oxime-functionalized polydiacetylene
PDA	polydiacetylene
PNT	peptide nanotube
SBA	mesoporous silica
SD	squaraine dye
SNP	silica nanoparticle
SWV	square-wave voltammetry
TBDMS	*tert*-butyldimethylsilyl

DISTRIBUTION LIST

The following individuals and organizations were provided with one electronic version of this report:

U.S. Army Combat Capabilities Development
Command Chemical Biological Center
(DEVCOM CBC)
FCDD-CBR-PD
ATTN: McGarvey, D.
       Morrissey, K.

Defense Threat Reduction Agency
DTRA-RD-IAR
ATTN: Pate, B.

DEVCOM CBC Technical Library
FCDD-CBR-L
ATTN: Foppiano, S.
      Stein, J.

Defense Technical Information Center
ATTN: DTIC OA